Love
That Lasts
a Lifetime

Love That Lasts a Lifetime

WYNONA FARQUHAR LEONARD

HAWTHORN BOOKS, INC.
W. Clement Stone, Publisher
NEW YORK

Library of Congress Catalog Card Number: 73–8487
ISBN: 0–8015–4702–4
1 2 3 4 5 6 7 8 9 10

To My Husband
Who Has Helped Me Learn
Love to Last a Lifetime

Contents

*Love
That Lasts
a Lifetime*

WHAT IS THIS THING
CALLED LOVE?

WE'RE IN LOVE, and everything will work out all right!"

"As long as we're in love, that is all that matters!"

"We love each other and nothing can ever come between us!"

Love is the only good reason for marriage, and nearly everyone thinks it is their reason, and yet . . .

Some of your married friends act disillusioned and impatient at times. That nice young couple down the street is getting a divorce. Weren't *they* in love once?

What is this "love" which works such magic? A delicious feeling? A state of ecstatic happiness? A thrilling emotion? Romantic love is all of these, and like the delicate, rosy balloon it resembles, romantic love can collapse from a pinprick of trouble.

But true love is strong; it grows, deepens, becomes ever more precious, so that in twenty years you may look back on your honeymoon and exclaim, "We thought we were in love then, but it was nothing compared to what we have now!"

True love lasts, if you nourish it, work at it, care for it. But sometimes couples mistake other emotions for love. Romance and infatuation deceive many. They are "in love with love" and idealize a companion into a life-long mate. Too late they learn that what they called love was only physical attraction or the excitement of becoming engaged and married because all their friends were.

Many people have tried to describe true love and there is a common theme running through all the definitions. You love when you accept a person for his own worth, not for what he does for you. You love when his happiness is as important to you as your own, and when you find *your* happiness in helping him be the kind of person he wishes to be.

True love holds fast through hardship and sorrow; it is man's greatest source of joy and strength; and when we love truly, we come closest to expressing in human nature that which is like to divine.

What is this true love? Alexander Magoun defines it as "the passionate and abiding desire on the part of two or more people to produce together the conditions under which each can be, and spontaneously express, his real self; to produce together an intellectual soil and emotional climate in which each can flourish, far superior to what either could achieve alone."*

How do you know if you have this kind of love?

Do you accept the other person as he is? If a girl loves a man who glories in physical activity as a farmer or athletic coach, she will not coax him to work in an office, for love accepts his real self. If a man loves a girl who is quiet and retiring, finding her joy in homemaking, he is not going to complain if she does not become a part of sophisticated, party-and-club-centered groups.

True love does create conditions for change and growth, for each of us has many potentialities and in the right soil and climate we may bring forth hidden

*Alexander Magoun, *Love and Marriage* (New York: Harper & Brothers, 1956), p. 7. Used by permission.

abilities. Love encourages and gives confidence, and in that atmosphere the loved one grows into his best self.

True love has concern for the welfare of the other; it means that his happiness is as important to you as your own. It means, moreover, that *you* find happiness in making it possible for him to be and do what he wishes.

Finally, when you love truly, you know you are being your real self, not putting on a front. Together you are more real, more complete, finer persons than either could be alone. One of my students wrote in a class paper:

That which I now have, and which I definitely believe to be love, started out no differently from any of the previous episodes—if anything, it started more slowly and at times was farthest from my mind. The realization finally came through to me that 'this was it' but it didn't have the fanfare and sureness about it that I had always expected would be there.

The first realization came when I found that I was not pretending and never had been. The whole time I was falling in love with someone I had not realized it. Thinking back now, it is evident that the times I dated my wife were the times I needed someone I could trust with that which I truly was and not the things I pretended to be under other circumstances.

IS OURS TRUE LOVE?

*W*HY DID YOU CHOOSE this particular partner? Is this really love, or are you in love with the idea of being in love and this person is available? What about him or her helps you to be your real self, and what about you helps him or her? For to love truly, you must meet each other's needs.

Just as your physical selves need food, water, air, and rest to be healthy, so your emotional selves have needs that must be met if you are to be emotionally healthy, happy individuals. Each of us needs to feel he belongs—is accepted, respected, and loved. Babies in institutions where every physical care is given literally sicken and die without TLC—tender, loving care—cuddling and crooning. Adults with no one to love and be loved by may survive, but they are apt to react by being hostile and aggressive or withdrawn and submissive. At worst, they fill the beds of mental hospitals.

Every human being has two basic emotional needs—for love and for significance, and perhaps the first is included in the latter. For to give and receive love is to know our life has meaning. The need for significance is the need to feel our life is worth something in this world, that it counts for more than "the grass of the field." Significance is so deep a need that it may be at the heart of religious longing.

Love is a law of human relationships as truly as gravity is a law of matter and electricity is a law of positive and negative charges. Humans must relate to each other with love, or destruction (meaning unhappiness, depression, hostility, hate) follows as surely as when laws are broken in the physical world.

How do you know if you have made the right choice? Ask yourself two questions, for upon truthful answers depends whether you will meet each other's needs for love and significance. Only if you do can you expect the emotional security that a truly fine marriage brings.

First: Is your love "true" or only "romance"? Do

you passionately desire to produce together the conditions under which you and your mate can be your real selves? You must know each other well enough to know what these conditions are.

Second: Do you get your significance from similar values? If the most important thing in life to one is prestige and material possessions, while to the other it is service to community welfare, neither can meet the other's need for support in producing conditions. If one finds satisfaction in having a house like a decorator's while the other wants to take in boys the parole officer is hunting a home for, they cannot possibly produce together conditions in which each finds significance.

The girl who feels that mothering children would be her most satisfying contribution to society would probably be miserable with a man who wanted his wife to be an expensively dressed accessory to display his business success.

The man whose real self is best expressed when teaching or doing youth work would get little help from a wife who craves financial ability in her husband.

If you do not treasure the same purposes in life, you will find it hard to love each other dearly. "Where our treasure is, there our heart is also."

These two emotional needs, for love and

significance, are the ones married lovers must fill for each other, and the husband or wife who does not support his or her mate emotionally is as guilty of non-support as if he would not provide food and she would not prepare it.

Questions as hard as these cannot be answered quickly; neither can the answers entirely be put into words. They take time spent together, observing, listening, feeling out attitudes and your own responses to them.

You need to explore the way each of you wants his needs met, and the possibility of your being able and happy to meet them.

That is one reason for engagement: to test your feelings and learn if you can communicate. Can you express how you feel, and can this partner tune in on your wave-length and respond to your messages?

THE ENGAGEMENT:
MAKING SURE

*W*HAT IS THE PURPOSE of an engagement? Is it to have the girl's picture in the society pages, to display the ring, to revel in parties and showers and congratulations? This part is exciting, but why should a couple who have decided they are right for each other put off marriage for months? Are engagements only a social custom?

Some are; those which are merely excuses for a social whirl and increased privileges of intimacy. But ideally, the engagement period can be most important to building a truly fine marriage. It can be the time for final testing of this vital decision, and a growing together in preparation for a new type of life. If engagements were properly used, there might be more broken ones, but there would be fewer broken marriages and the latter are far more tragic.

The engagement is a time of transition from the carefree days of dating and courtship to the responsibility of founding a new unit of society. You announce your plans to the community and seek group approval and acceptance. It is more than your personal affair when you propose to take on marriage responsibility, because society has a stake in the type of home and family you establish.

This growing together period involves at least four tasks: getting a physical examination, getting used to being a part of each other's family, preparing to assume mature responsibility, and learning to think as a pair.

The physical examination should check on present state of health and inquire into possible hereditary defects that may require special care when children are expected (such as a diabetic condition or RH incompatibility). A genital examination and opportunity to ask questions about the physical side of sex and methods of family planning acceptable to both should be included. If there is any indication that either cannot have children, you should both know it and decide how you will adjust to such a possibility.

Years ago, young people used to marry within their own little neighborhoods, where families were much alike; now we are such a mobile people that there are great differences in family customs, and it takes more time to grow into pair solidarity. Knowing and establishing a friendly relationship with each other's family is part of engagement. You do "marry the family," because what your mate is like depends a great deal on how his family has shaped him. As you love him or her, you should love the ones who helped build this personality. At the same time, you two must now begin to break the cords that bind you to your old homes and feel that "family" now means, primarily, the two of you.

Frequently a young couple has been more dependent upon parents than they realize. Now the girl must learn homemaking skills so she can manage a household capably and smoothly. The man takes his work more seriously, begins an insurance program (if he has not before), plans a budget with his fiancée. You begin to consider community obligations as well as amusements.

Finally, you begin to think in terms of "we" rather than "I." You build a "pair feeling" a little like the feeling you may have had with a debate or tennis partner who was just right for you. But this pair feeling is not in *one* shared interest, but about nearly every phase of your life—your ideas of a home, your friends, your recreation, your vocation.

These are some of the steps from single independence to married interdependency which should be taken during your engagement.

Turning from the "growing together," let's look at the "testing" side of your engagement. You are making the final test of the proposition that you should spend the rest of your lives together. You want to discover any major difficulties now, because marriage is not a reform school and you have no right to try to change another's personality. (You *can* each work at adjusting your own so that you bring out the best in each other.)

Perhaps you sense that real feelings are being masked by conventional politeness. How do you get behind the mask to the real person? This is the time to do less of the ordinary dating activities such as parties, dancing, or movies, and try to share as many different situations as possible, letting you two know each other under all conditions. Try working on something together, such as furnishings for your home. Spend time in each other's homes helping with daily tasks. Learn new skills together.

This is the time to get the feel of family backgrounds, to explore personal habits—such as promptness, orderliness, patience, endurance, moods—and ask yourself how important these are. This is not a question of "How does he or she suit me?" but "How do we suit each other?"

Engagement is the time to test your ability to solve problems together. You discuss a place to live, how important spending or saving money is. Will you try to establish a high standard of living at once or deny yourselves now for a better future? You discuss children—number and spacing. (You may change your minds on this later, but you'll change them together.)

More important, you'll discuss your theories on disciplining and guiding children. This is one of the best ways of learning to know each other, for it brings to light what each feels is important in character. You will decide the part religious observance will play in your lives.

Such discussions are a test of your ability to reach decisions that are satisfactory to both. If you fail, don't rush into marriage thinking that will solve differences. Take time, postpone marriage until you can find a solution or agree to live with certain differences without quarreling. Call off the marriage rather than leave serious questions unsettled. An engagement "broken by mutual consent," as all should be so far as the public is informed, is only a minor disturbance in life's voyage. A broken marriage can wreck two lives.

Quite naturally, there is more feeling of freedom in expressing love once a couple is formally engaged, and with some this leads to the question of how far to go. The "just as good as married" argument is used to justify intimacies that may leave one or both feeling guilty and take the luster from marriage.

Ask yourselves if the demand for premarital sex isn't a childish matter of wanting what you want when you want it. May it indicate a lack of trust in the other's love and a desire for reassurance—and even then, not being able to believe? Does it mean a lack of confidence in self, a fear "Am I really lovable?" Is it not a sign of immaturity to be unable to postpone present pleasure for future happiness? The ultimate expression of love is so wonderful that it deserves to be set apart as the consummation of the wedding ceremony.

Can you talk to each other about how you feel about chastity? You should be able to, and to help each other achieve what your best judgment tells you. Plan your time together so there will not be too much opportunity for temptation, for you really have much homework to do to get ready for this great adventure.

Many ask how long an engagement should be. Of course there is no ideal length, but studies do show that happy marriages are much more prevalent among those who have been engaged a year or longer. Mere length is no guarantee of happiness, but the quality of thoughtful preparation is. It takes time to talk out all the angles of life together; it takes time to learn about personality as it comes to light under different situations; it takes time to find if you have deep companionship, if you need the same intellectual soil and emotional climate and passionately desire to create it together.

Accept the fact that you will have doubts now and then. Ask yourself which result from a reluctance to give up carefree singleness; which are caused by a yearning for some impossible dream-image of your adolescent days? And remember that life is a series of choices that involve giving up one good for the sake of a more worthwhile one.

THE WEDDING

*W*EDDINGS ARE EVENTS that brides (and their mothers) have planned for and dreamt about from little-girlhood. Grooms seem, mostly, to endure them—because "women are like that" and a man likes to make them happy.

Of course you can have an impersonal ceremony in a judge's office, which is perfectly legal, but it lacks the beauty and solemnity of one shared by your family and friends who love you and are happy in your happiness. Even statistics favor the home or church wedding. One study of marriages begun with a civil ceremony found two out of three ending in divorce.*

*Locke, *Predicting Adjustment in Marriage* (New York, Henry Holt & Co., 1951), p. 238.

Granted, there is no magic in the vows or the place, but the ceremony performed by a justice of the peace is more apt to be an impulsive, ill-considered act than one approved by family and friends.

On the other hand, some church ceremonies are little more than fashionable pageants, carefully staged, costumed, and decorated. The real purpose gets lost amid the flowers and gowns and reception gaiety. The couple may well be so concerned with giving a perfect performance that it is hard for them to keep their minds on the vows they are repeating after the minister.

Your wedding should be a sacramental act, a making holy of the step you are taking, lifting and dedicating your life together. Beautiful it should be, and you will want your friends to share this moment with you, but don't let the meaning be lost in the mechanics.

Some time before the wedding, you two should have an unhurried conference with your minister or priest. Nearly all pastors will use this opportunity to help a couple understand the sacred nature of marriage, of which the ceremony is only the beginning. You will want to know the wording of the vows you will take and think about their meaning. You may decide to memorize them and make the beautiful and moving commitment of love which abides in sickness and in health, for better or worse, for richer or poorer, so long as you both shall live, directly to each other.

No matter how simple or elaborate, how small or large, your wedding should mean that before God and the community of friends, you are pledging a lasting relationship. It is more than a contract, though it is governed by law. It is more than social custom, though the family in some form has existed throughout the history of man. It is more than a partnership, though a good marriage is that, too.

Marriage is the deepest, most meaningful relation of life, and in this it resembles religion. Marriage, like religion, is a commitment of one's self to a way of life. Marriage commits the mates to bringing out the best in themselves and each other.

THE HONEYMOON

$\mathcal{H}$ONEYMOON seems to mean, to most people, an interlude of romantic bliss—a kind of never-never land from which you return to practical daily living with a dull thud. We hear folks say "The honeymoon is over" as if joy and delight in each other were ended with marriage becoming just a convenient arrangement for room, board, and laundry.

Is this true? Cannot the honeymoon be, instead, the prologue to a new life that becomes more satisfying each year, not an anticlimax to those first days? This is what it should be, and will be, if you are prepared to make it so.

What about planning the honeymoon? Will this take the romance from it? Should the young husband "surprise" his bride? Hardly! Planning for it together is practice in making decisions. You learn to work out a solution pleasing to both. If his idea of perfect bliss is a packtrip through a primitive forest and she is terrified by a screech owl, she might spend her honeymoon adjusting to smoky campfires instead of to her husband.

If you have never stayed at a swank resort hotel, you may have to give more thought to how much to tip the doorman, what others are thinking of you, and what the stay is doing to your savings, than to the enjoyment of each other and your marriage. You should decide on a place where both will be at ease.

A honeymoon is not a "wedding trip," not a crowded schedule of sightseeing, long, hard drives and entertainment. It should be a time to get away from every person who knows you, for complete privacy from the curious and interfering. It is a time to get used to each other in this new physical intimacy in which two people from different families suddenly begin to live together, eating, sleeping, dressing and undressing together.

It is a period in which there should be time enough to talk with no clock to watch; a period to savor and enjoy; to let your lover share your thoughts and emotions when you see a sunrise over a mountain, watch the moon shimmer on a lake, or look out upon the hurrying crowds of a city street. It is an unveiling of spirit as well as body.

Wherever the honeymoon is spent, it should be in as pleasant surroundings as possible, though that does not mean swank or luxury. Finances must be planned so there is no worry about affording it. Decide together what you can spend, find the best spot you can for that amount, and forget money. Relax from the wedding excitement and enjoy each other.

Learning to express love sexually begins during the honeymoon. We hear much about lack of knowledge about sex; actually many folks know too much that isn't so! No subject is so moss-encrusted with misinformation gleaned from bull sessions, hush-hush folklore, and pseudo-scientific magazine articles as sex is. Fortunately, texts on marriage and sex manuals are available in most libraries. The doctor to whom you go for your premarital examination, or your minster, can refer you to accurate material.

However, more important than physiological knowledge is attitude, and this has so often been conditioned by poor childhood training that probably no other one subject has been responsible for so many emotional cripples.

Older generations thought they were protecting children by teaching them to regard sex as shameful and dirty, or to fear it. They felt guilty about it themselves. Whatever your past teaching, now is the time to get a wholesome attitude and a good way to begin is to be honest with yourself.

How do you feel about sex? How do you want to feel? What should you do to feel the way you want to? Because sex is such a strong instinct, it, like all impulses, needs control. The old way was control by fear of punishment and shame, associating sex with guilt. Or it was something to snigger at, a vulgar act to be indulged secretly because it was fun, but not to be admitted.

Fear has been linked with sex; girls have been taught to fear pain, fear pregnancy, fear they are coarse if they even admit sexual attraction. In reaction, some have gone to the other extreme, glorifying sexual allure.

Hostility and aggression have been linked with sex. Men may express anger and resentment in sex as something vengeful they do *to* women. It may be a way of assuring themselves they are superior or important.

To some, sex may mean nothing more than an act of physical satisfaction. To some, it may be good only as the means to procreation of children. But it may and *should* mean the ultimate expression of physical and emotional unity between a loving man and woman.

How do you *want* to feel about it? Surely not fear or guilt or aggression, but that it is right and good and joyful. It should be controlled because its right use is worth it. What can you do to feel this way?

Be honest with yourself and admit what you do feel and try to understand why, for when a false attitude is brought out into the open and the reason you have it becomes clear, it shrivels away. Why should anyone think a God-given instinct evil? It is not sex, but the use we make of it, that is good or evil. Used for selfish exploitation of another, it is evil; used as the joyous expression of spiritual oneness in marriage, it is good and beautiful.

What has this to do with the honeymoon? You bring to this first union your emotional attitudes, and since intercourse is so charged with emotion, its success is influenced by these attitudes. If lovers can talk over these feelings before marriage, they will be getting practice in the art of communication and learning to share ideas about values.

However, there are facts that both need to know. One is the difference in sex needs. The man's drive is direct, physical, quickly satisfied, and not so dependent upon setting the scene. The woman's role is response and greatly affected by surroundings, emotional atmosphere, and psychological factors. She needs to be roused gently, wooed with word and caress, to feel sure and safe in the man's devotion. This is the time for tender words and assurance; she must feel herself so deeply loved that she can give herself gladly. Ideally, the young husband should slow his own eagerness and quicken hers so they may reach a climax together.

This may not happen at first; sex is a skill and an art to be learned together. In these early days, both are apt to be keyed to concert pitch, yet with underlying anxieties. With real love and understanding, mates will not expect perfection at once; they will not be upset, critical, or disappointed. They will know it takes time to learn.

There has been much written of recent years about the necessity of the woman reaching an orgasm—in fact, many writers have gone to the extreme of making that the criterion of married happiness. They write as if proper physical techniques are all that is necessary for a good marriage and a wife is happy in proportion to the number of orgasms she has.

This is highly questionable. For one thing, too much concern about it may distract from the relaxed joy of the union. For another, there may be times when the wife has little desire, yet can be happy to give herself to her husband as she would do other loving acts to please him. This is not the old idea of the wife's duty to submit to her husband's demands. Rather, when they can talk freely and frankly, there is joy just in the giving; if she reaches a climax, well and good—if not, there is no frustration.

When should the first intercourse take place? There is no law that says it must be the wedding night. After all the excitement and nervous tension of the wedding, plus some travel, this may not be the best time. It should come when both want it and are ready, physically and emotionally.

Some young husbands have been so in-doctrinated with the idea of women's reluctance that they have been shocked if their wives indicated they welcomed intercourse. This is a hangover from the idea that sex is shameful and that women, being of finer clay, merely submit. Actually, when good communication exists between mates, each welcomes the confidence shown in letting their wishes be known to each other.

Sex is normal, joyful, good; it means many things from fun and comradeship and teasing playfulness to sympathetic reassurance and comfort. Most of all it means love. It is not the be-all or end-all of marriage, not a sophisticated technique, but the happy accompaniment of real love which is acting naturally.

The honeymoon is the kindergarten of a life education in deepening devotion. As that grows, so will joy and satisfaction in sexual expression grow through the years.

HOW WILL YOU PLAY
YOUR NEW ROLES?

*W*HEN YOU ARE BACK from your honeymoon, sharing a home, each taking responsibility for certain duties in that home, you see each other in different roles from those of lover and sweetheart. You are a new family, husband and wife.

How do you expect a husband or wife to act? What should a family be like? How should you and your mate play these new roles?

Grandma knew just what was expected of her as a wife. She should bake, cook, raise a garden and can the surplus, do the sewing and laundry, sweep, scrub, do a little church work and occasionally have company. She expected to obey her husband but she knew her work was absolutely essential if the household was to eat and be decently clothed. She felt significant in her job.

Grandpa knew what a husband should be and do. He was very much the head of the house. He worked and made money and spent it; he was kind to his wife, even if firm, and laid down the law for the children when she needed a strong hand with them. Being a man meant that he had more experience and knew more about the world than she did so it did not occur to him to consult with her on decisions. This role of authority fulfilled his need for significance.

There used to be "woman's work" and "man's work" and either lost face, was not quite so much of a man, nor so respected as a woman, if they stepped out of traditional roles. Now boys and girls are educated alike, participate together in sports and recreation, work together in nearly every occupation. You expect this feeling of equality and companionship to carry over into marriage, but you may face two problems here that probably didn't trouble your grandparents.

One arises because you may still carry with you, from your own families, many of the ideas of the traditional husband-wife relationship; the other arises from the fact that men and women *are* equal, but *different* and you may tend to forget the difference in emphasizing the equality.

Each of you brings into marriage a mental picture of what it is like, based on your own family since that is the only one you "feel." You know about others intellectually, but all your *emotional* responses are tied up with the family life you have lived. If it was unhappy, you may be determined that you will do just the opposite in every area you recall with pain; if it was happy, you may look askance at any family procedure different from that which was pleasant at home.

Perhaps Jeff came from a traditional type family where father was decidedly the head; he handled the money, he solved the problems, he made the decisions. Jeff's mother liked it that way; she was happiest caring for domestic affairs and was glad to be spared other responsibility, content to carry out her husband's decisions unquestionably.

If Jeff's new wife, Carole, has had some experience in handling her own money, if her father and mother talked over together all family questions and made decisions jointly, even including the children in some discussions, she may well feel frustrated and think Jeff is overbearing and domineering if he is a husband like *his* father, making decisions on his own.

Yet Jeff feels he is merely taking the responsibility a mature man should, sparing his wife. To talk over problems with her may seem to Jeff like weakness. To him, it may be less than manly to "burden" his wife with what he feels are his responsibilities.

Perhaps Carole's mother paid the bills and balanced the joint checkbook each month. She was a good manager and an efficient purchasing agent and it worked out well for her to assume this part of the family duties. When Jeff insists on doing this, Carole is afraid he doesn't trust her judgment. The bills are paid and Jeff doesn't complain about them, but her feeling of worth is threatened and she fights back by calling Jeff stingy and domineering.

Jeff's mother picked up after her men and they never helped with housework. When Carole expects Jeff to hang away his clothes or help clear the table, Jeff is afraid he is being henpecked and resists. He really wouldn't mind helping, but "it's the principle of the thing." What is a wife for? He's worked all day, earning a living; housework is her job! So he calls Carole "bossy" and retreats into sulky silence behind his newspaper.

What are these two actually feeling? Fear! Fear that each is threatened by the other; he in his strong manliness, the image he has of himself as the head, provider, protector of the home; she in her image of herself as the partner, shoulder-to-shoulder companion, trusted and helped with running the house. Each is afraid his worth is not recognized. Their images of husband and wife roles are entirely different.

What do they want to feel? Recognized and accepted as worthwhile, capable adults. They need to be assured, each by the other, that they are significant. Not in so many words, but through appreciation, they want to know they are doing their jobs.

The other problem you may face is the idea some people have of equality of men and women, and the actual fact of their inborn differences. There is no conflict if you realize that difference does not mean inferiority or superiority. Each has a unique contribution to make, and they should complement and fulfill each other, not be rivals.

Because, at one time, women were regarded as attractive and appealing, but rather useless except as they contributed to the comfort of men, the ladies rebelled and set out to prove their ability. They did it in the only way they could, by doing the things men considered important. They took on the men in their own fields, in factories, business, the professions.

The pendulum swung to the far extreme, and the feminist movement insisted that women were no different than men, except a little better.

Psychiatrists say that many women as they enter the competitive world of business, adopt masculine characteristics of aggressiveness. They tend to carry this aggressiveness over into marriage and the family. They compete with their husbands in providing for and being the head of the family. They want to make, rather than share in, decisions.

In turn, husbands either compete with their wives for dominance, making a battleground of the home, or tend to adopt the feminine role of being passive and submissive. It is not an accident that much of our humor caricatures the meek, slightly dumb husband and domineering wife.

In either case, both husband and wife are unhappy. Woman is by nature planned for the receptive, passive role; man the aggressive, active one. Woman bears and nurtures the children and makes a haven for the man; man provides for, defends, protects the women and children.

If they reverse roles, the wife finds she is not satisfied with her husband and she does not respect him. Her essentially feminine nature is being denied. Unconsciously she is missing her deep need to play the receptive role. Her husband lacks respect for himself and misses the significance he should get from the protective, positive role, and he, too, is dissatisfied—not being and expressing his real self.

Your generation has to learn to weave together the equality of men's and women's intellectual companionship and the emotional satisfaction which comes from playing their instinctive male and female roles. Both sexes have the same basic emotional needs for love and significance, but they must fulfill those needs in different ways or they will compete with, instead of complementing, each other.

Do not be discouraged if you do not constantly feel at a peak of closeness. All life has rhythm, ebb and flow. There is a dormant time in winter before the return of spring. All you need is the confidence that love is there in enough supply to carry through and flourish again in spring.

QUARRELING—
OR COMMUNICATION?

As YOU FEEL OUT your new roles as man and wife, there are apt to be some differences of opinion about how these roles should be played. If you can tell each other the truth about what you are feeling without varnishing it or trying to make your feelings into some special virtue, you can communicate.

There is a great difference between Carole's saying, "You're domineering and stingy! You treat me like a child! You don't trust me!" and saying, "Having my own checkbook would make me feel like your partner. Having to ask you for money makes me feel childish." Or, "Not knowing just how we stand financially makes it hard for me to plan what we can afford."

There is a great difference between "I can't stand a bossy female! You're not going to henpeck me into being a household servant!" and "Mom never expected Dad to help with the dishes and it doesn't seem like man's work to me" or "I'm awfully tired tonight and I've been looking forward to the big chair and the hi-fi."

Two of these retorts attack the other person: "*You* are stingy!" "*You* are bossy and henpecking!" They tear down a person's precious sense of personal worth or significance, create doubts as to his being loved or lovable. These are quarrels.

The other remarks attack the problem, not the person. They bring into the open the real source of dissatisfaction. Each tells the other how he feels, and from there lovers can go on to work out a solution. They show confidence that the other wants to understand and will try to produce the conditions in which each can be himself. This is communication.

It is better to bring unhappiness out into the open. Smothering it, playing the silent martyr, is no virtue. Within, like steam, pressure is building up that may explode over a minor incident or, even worse, may fester and infect the whole relationship with resentment.

In the explosion, words come pouring out that hurt and wound. Even though, with the return of calmness, we know they were not meant and we wish to recall them, a scar may remain. The festering kind of resentment turns into unconscious hate, expressed in little unloving words and acts until the couple is so far apart it seems a hopeless task to get together again.

Better to get the real problem into the open. Told to a mate who listens with love, confident that that love is equal to making things right between them, it can be worked out.

True lovers do not want to win victories over their mates. They want to solve the problems that separate them.

MONEY

*M*ONEY IS A STUMBLING BLOCK in many marriages and one that may take a long time to remove. The amount seems to have little to do with happiness. The Smiths may feel pinched on a large income while the Browns live happily on half that amount. Studies show that happiness and money are related at only two points: that there be agreement on how it is spent and that there be some regularity of income, however small. Insurance and some savings for emergencies give freedom from worry.

It is a shared attitude toward money that keeps it from being a problem. Money can mean so many different things. Try asking a group of people the first word that comes into their minds when they hear the word *money*. Answers will range from "Trouble," "Worry," "Salary" to "Security," "Gifts," "Fun."

Money is freedom of choice to select those things that are important to you. To some, it may be to set a good table; to others, tickets to concerts and the theater though meals may be plain. Some choose clothes, club memberships, cars, while others prize books, education, travel, contributions.

After the basic necessities of life are cared for, the way you use your money indicates what your values are, and this shows how well suited a couple are to each other. Are your values, those things for which you will give up other goods, the same? How do you satisfy your need for significance, from without or within?

Much is being said about materialism and status. Advertisers play upon the human desire for status, assuring readers that owning a certain car, certain furs, an "all gas" or "all electric" kitchen, a speed boat, a patio with barbecue—*this* will make you secure and happy. All of which is described in the old phrase, "keeping up with the Joneses." And too many people have heeded the urging of the persuaders, falling for the enticements of easy credit and installment buying until they are burdened with debts while their status symbols bring them nothing but strain and worry.

Young couples need to talk seriously about what is important to them. Shall your significance come from what you buy? Shall you have friends in for a homecooked dinner and cards or go nightclubbing? Shall you spend your leisure time in civic and church organizations, or social groups, or find friends in both circles? The importance to marriage is that husband and wife agree on which they choose.

Money should be fun; you should manage it rather than having it manage you. How can you have enough to make choices with? How can you avoid worry about it?

Sit down together and plan. Put down first the fixed expenses—those that must be paid, such as taxes, insurance (car, life, health, property), interest or payments on debts and mortgage, etc. Then set aside some (10 percent if possible) for an emergency fund to take care of the unexpected, such as sudden loss of income or a big repair bill. This fund should be built up until it equals two, or better, three months' salary, then just maintained at that level. Estimate day by day expenses: shelter (unless that is under fixed expenses), food, clothing, contributions, gifts, transportation, recreation, etc. This division may vary greatly. The more skillful person may stretch dollars to make the difference between being comfortable or pinched in this area of life.

Somewhere set aside something for personal allowances for each, to spend with no questions asked.

Then comes the fun part. Put down all the things you want in the dream future, such as a new house, education for children, a vacation cottage, a trip abroad. Mark this "Future" and decide how much to allot to it. Then put down the things you want and need soon, such as appliances, new furniture, tools, and note what each will cost. Arrange them in order of importance to you and plan how much you can put away each payday for your first want. You'll have fun twice—as you save toward your goal and when you reach it. Then start on your second want. As soon as children are old enough, they may be included in the family planning councils. Their wants should be considered, but they also learn that Dad and Mother have needs and wants, too, and they can mature as they learn the satisfaction of helping others attain *their* desires.

Many people won't wait—they buy at once, and "put aside" by going into the store and handing over the monthly or weekly payments. They say they *have* to save that way. Maybe—but the cost of having someone *make* you do what you should comes high, for carrying charges are mighty high interest. Most of those revolving or budget charge accounts bring the store 18 percent or more. Can you afford to pay that kind of interest?

Installment buying may be necessary for a young couple for some major needs when they get started, such as a stove or washing machine. A good rule is never to buy on installment anything that lasts less than three years, make as large a down payment as possible, and never commit more than 10 percent of your income to installment payments.

WHEN YOU BECOME
THREE—OR MORE

*T*HE DESIRE FOR CHILDREN was listed as the principal reason for marriage by 10 percent of the young people interviewed in one survey. Certainly it is one of the greatest joys of marriage for nearly everyone. It is one of the things to be discussed during engagement to make sure there is some similarity of attitude toward parenthood. Deciding when and how many involves acceptance of planned parenthood and a common attitude toward birth control.

When? There is considerable evidence to indicate it is well to give yourselves a year or so to adjust to each other before adding the adjustment of a baby.

There may be the question of the wife working for a time until some specific goal is reached, such as payment of college debts or a down payment on a house. But it is possible to put off having a baby for too long, always waiting for an ever-higher standard of living when you actually could manage very well.

How many? How many can you sincerely welcome? Every child has a right to be wanted. It is a sin against a human spirit to be brought into the world if he is not going to find loving welcome to give him the feeling of acceptance and worth so essential to growing into a fine person.

Having children is not something to be undertaken because society expects it, or because your friends are having them, or because babies are so cute. If the latter is the reason, better get a kitten; when it becomes a cat, it at least can take care of itself when you are tired of it.

Sometimes a father is left out in the months of looking forward to a baby's birth, but he shouldn't be. He should be in on everything, planning the layette and nursery, the prenatal classes, the mother's hopes and fears. By sharing these, he can reassure her and keep her morale high.

Some hospitals let fathers stay with their wives, at least during the first stages of labor, and surely if ever there is a time when a wife wants her husband close, it is while she is going through this most wonderful experience of life. There are many crude jokes and cartoons about father pacing the floor of the waiting room, but they are not funny. This is his baby, too, and he shouldn't feel pushed aside.

When the new family comes home is no time for him to abdicate to an all-woman team, either, even if it consists of his wife and mother or mother-in-law. He should be part of this new situation. It is the most satisfying, most exciting interest he and his wife can share, and Dad should be learning parenthood right along with Mother.

Babies need to feel the security that only a father gives and which, in turn, keeps the father from having that "second fiddle" feeling entirely possible for him to get when his wife is absorbed in this new person.

As babies grow, the question of discipline comes up. Too many people confuse discipline with punishment. A child has the same emotional needs as an adult, for love and significance, but the latter, to a child, means only that his parents accept him, like him, want him. That gives him the security of knowing he has a place in the world. The baby's needs must be met in a way and at a level he can feel.

The tiny baby gets this from the security of having his needs for food and warmth and cuddling supplied. As he grows, he needs to know that he is accepted and loved, no matter what mistakes he makes. He cannot be permitted to act in uncontrolled, unsocial ways, but he can understand that it is the acts, not his personality, that are bad. He can feel that you have confidence he is essentially good and *can* learn to act acceptably.

Saying "You make me tired" attacks him. "Your crying makes me tired" condemns the deed, not the doer and lets him know what is wrong. "You are a bad boy" attacks him. "Tearing a book is bad" pinpoints the act.

"It is bad to get angry" confuses a child, because anger is an instinctive reaction, not a deliberate one. "It is bad to hurt people when you are angry" helps him realize he must learn to work off his anger in constructive ways.

When punishment is necessary, it should be the natural consequence of the wrong act—you punish the act, not the personality of the child. Making him stay in the house because he went into the street shows him he must earn the right to play outdoors by obeying safety rules. To take away his dessert has nothing to do with teaching right behavior.

Most of all, you need to remember that your job is to make yourselves unnecessary—that is, to help your child become a person ready to stand alone and make his contribution to the world in his own way. The definition of love applies here, for you will want to create the conditions in which he can be and express his real self—and to do that, he must learn to take responsibility as he shows he is ready.

Practically everyone expects to get some training for whatever job he undertakes, except parenthood. Husbands and wives go to bridge classes or take golf lessons together, yet few take classes or read books on child guidance. You who have read this far about marriage are probably the kind of people who will find satisfaction in studying together to be good parents.

THE DILEMMA OF
MODERN MATES

*T*HE NEED FOR ASSURANCE of love and significance is apt to be keenest right at the time, early in marriage, when each is least able to meet it. Both husband and wife may be so concerned with their own problems that they are less sensitive to their mate's. They are separated all day into two different worlds and not aware of the pressures on the other. This is your modern dilemma.

There are going to be many days when a young mother wonders if she is anything more than a cook, laundress, and nursemaid—if she will ever again have time for reading or tennis or dancing. She looks forward to her husband's homecoming as a chance for renewal of some of the romance and gaiety of dating days; she wants to go out and enjoy adult conversation and forget diapers and spilled food and muddy shoes.

Meanwhile, this is the time the husband is working hardest to establish himself in his chosen field and when he is least secure there. There is strain from competition for promotion; there may be criticism from supervisors above, frustration from inefficiency on the part of those for whom he is responsible. This is why men get ulcers. It is hard to feel much personal satisfaction from many modern organizational jobs, yet they take great quantities of a man's nervous energy.

The husband looks forward to coming home and shutting the door on the world of battling. He wants a haven of peace and quiet. Yet this is the very time his wife is most apt to be tired from babytending and the thousands of little demands that nibble away at time and energy but seem such a trivial way to spend it. She may greet her husband with demands for sympathy, for help with the children, or complaints about the neighbors.

Each needs support from the other; they want assurance of their own worth, though they may not recognize that this is their need. Can his need to get away from people and hers to seek stimulation from people be reconciled?

Some women solve this by going to work outside the home even while their children are small—though they may not consciously recognize just why. One said, "My husband never seemed to think what I did amounted to much until I got a job and he saw that others thought my work was worth paying for."

Aside from a sentimental, Mother's-Day-card sort of gesture, society doesn't pay much respect to the job of being a wife and mother. Certainly we act as if the doings and opinions of the smart business woman, the actress, the author, or professional woman are more important.

Trying to get two or three small boys to quit fighting over who uses the wagon and who the trike or scooter, and steering them all into playing "parade"; getting your little girl and her best friend to be kind to the scraggly child down the street as they walk to school—these may not rate you a notice among civic welfare leaders, but the boys are learning cooperation and the girls to see beyond outward appearance.

Good homes with well-loved children growing up in them are the basic unit of national life. Whether or not our nation shall be one of high political integrity depends on the moral fiber of its citizens, and that is built in the home. But it takes a sense of humor and a lot of maturity to keep such lofty ends in perspective when your days are occupied with heating bottles, struggling with snowsuits, and listening to squabbles.

Most of all, it takes a lot of appreciation from a husband and his cooperation in planning so a mother can get away from the house now and then and keep in touch with the interests for which she was educated. Both need to remember that baby-tending is only a small portion of family life and that there will be decades of time for other interests after the children are gone.

Husbands, too, have emotional needs. One said, "The lack of something to feel important about is almost the greatest tragedy a man may have." Modern life intensifies this lack. Men no longer get it from being an authoritarian head of the family, or, if they seek it by being so, the family suffers. There is less opportunity to find importance in their work, because the majority of young husbands are not working for themselves but are parts of an impersonal organization.

An aggressive, demanding wife continues the stress and tearing down process a man may endure at work. A loving wife builds him up. She wants the children to understand what Daddy's work does for people; she emphasizes his importance as a husband and father. A man needs recognition and appreciation. He needs to know his wife is proud of him, loves and trusts him, that he is necessary to her.

Mates need to help each other plan—for her to keep up her musical interest with a choir—for him to get away for an evening of bowling. Just knowing that the other understands that you need such changes, means a lot.

When Jeff notices that the house is freshly cleaned, when he says, "How do you manage to accomplish so much?" or "I'm sure you'd do a good job as chairman of that committee," Carole knows he sees her to be a worthwhile person.

When Carole thanks Jeff for holding her chair; says, "He took me to a movie," "He bought me a stove," "Jeff thinks—" instead of taking courtesies, entertainment, or support for granted, she is putting into words her attitude of appreciation. She shows that his opinion counts with her, building his significance and thus giving him emotional security.

Good marriage gives confidence to the partners. The husband's masculine strength supports his wife when the going gets tough; her feminine dependence builds him up, and her love and tenderness reassure him.

FUN OR JUST DUTY?

*D*ATING, COURTSHIP AND ENGAGE-
MENT are fun. Should the fun go out of life when two
people have chosen each other and made that choice
final by marriage? What was it about that
preparatory part that kept you both so happy?

"Romance" you say—the thrill and excitement of
the unknown, the adventurous, the new. You were
exploring a new personality, each looking forward to
a new adventure in living. Romance is not enough to
get married on, but it *can* give some spice to life after
the ceremony.

Now that you have settled down you have the safe, secure feeling of being sure you are loved, but you sometimes want some fun, something different. One of you is going to have to break through routine and plan for it. Perhaps the wife may set the scene with an especially nice candle-lit dinner with the best china and her next-to-best dress. He may bring home a little surprise or call from the office for a "date" to the movies.

You used to plan to make dates fun; it takes some planning for recreation and social life. Friends don't just happen. You make them and make some effort to keep friendships living. Trying new skills, sports, and games gives adventure to ordinary days, and the new activities you add as the children grow can be exciting—if you take that attitude toward them.

Marriage and a family can be dreary duty or fun; it depends on your attitude. Ironing a husband's shirt is menial drudgery or "love made visible." Children are responsibilities to be fed, clothed, nursed, and educated, but they are also new people to be loved and enjoyed, to help you see the world all new again through their eyes.

The Smiths take their children for granted. They answer questions if asked, and see that the children lack for nothing, but they do not particularly enjoy them. The Browns make an effort to let their children know they are appreciated as part of the family circle. They talk with them at the table; they let them share their grown-up parties when they entertain, if only by meeting the guests and taking their wraps. They put the children's crayoned paper hearts or pumpkin faces or turkeys on the family table on holidays.

Which young generation will remember home with warm pleasure and want homes and families for themselves? It *is* work to get material together to make May baskets or valentines. It messes up the kitchen to color Easter eggs and birthday parties can be exhausting. It is simpler to visit the corner drug store and buy the valentines and baskets and candy eggs, but the fun of working together with a child, which makes him feel he is important to you, is lost.

Romance involves some sentimental attachment to repeating pleasures—"our song," "our" special hill or beach or moonlit view. And traditions in marriage can have that same sentimental value.

Children like to repeat what they have found pleasant. They want to return to the same vacation spot, to have the same Sunday night supper, to hear the same stories over, to make the same jokes. It gives them the same secure feeling that old grads have when they thrill to the college song. Adults call this tradition. It is a good thing to hand down some traditions from the two parent families and to build a few new ones in your own.

There is emotional security for both parents and children in family customs. Knowing that there will be a birthday cake with candles on your special day; that there will be a story at bedtime; that the same treasured old ornaments will reappear to be put on the Christmas tree; that Mom will be there when you get home from school, unless she has told you beforehand—this being able to count on something makes all of us feel better able to cope with this world in which so much is uncertain.

In one family with little money but much love, each person always told the birthday child one nice thing about him and made a wish for him. In another, Sunday afternoons were set aside for "just the family" to go to a park or museum, to pop corn or show home pictures. Family reunions featured a play written and acted by the young cousins.

Social poverty is almost worse than financial, for it starves the human spirit. Overcoming it requires only the will to do and appreciate the little pleasures of daily living. Refusal to make the effort for happiness is "the will to be dreary."

THE PLACE OF
RELIGION IN YOUR
MARRIAGE AND
FAMILY

*W*HERE DOES RELIGION FIT into the life of the family? Some popular articles make it merely another technique for togetherness, as in the platitude "Families that pray together stay together." Manufacturers of sporting goods substitute "play" for "pray" with nearly as much justification.

Others stress the importance of attending church together as a family and quote statistics on the solidarity of families which do. Again, this is regarding religion as a tool for serving family unity. It might be interesting to make a similar study of families who regularly attend a symphony series together.

Truly religious families *will* pray together and go to church together, but if there is no spiritual unity in the family, the outward act has no meaning.

Religion is not a tool or a technique to serve the family. It is not supernatural justification to reinforce parents' authority. It is not membership in a religious organization. Religion is the way we live because we believe certain things are true and family living is one way we express the truths we believe.

These truths are values—things we believe are so important we will sacrifice other desires to preserve them. Nearly all religions believe the basis of the se values is a Spirit which originates and conserves them, and this Spirit is called God. Values include such things as truth, kindness, freedom, concern for others, friendliness, forgiveness; most of all, love. Since we think of these as characteristics of the Spirit we call God, we call them spiritual values.

What we believe about God and the purpose of human life profoundly influences our attitudes and actions. This is our yardstick for determining right and wrong, if we are truly religious. If we believe that God loves us, we can apply our definition of love here; then we see the world, with its opportunity to choose good or evil, as the soil and climate God created in which we can express our real selves by the choices we make. If we believe we are children of God (have some of his spirit within us) our real selves *can* turn what happens to us, hard though it may be, to a good end.

A loving wife or husband, a loving parent, sees mate or child as precious because of spiritual potential. God has given us freedom to choose what we shall do with our lives, so a truly loving person does not try to force or change others but to cherish and encourage the good in them that it may grow.

Keeping spiritual values in mind is not easy. Modern advertising uses all the resources of psychology to discover motives and needs and appeal to them to create wants for the articles they offer for sale. The constant pressure to conform to what friends and neighbors think is important to have is hard to resist. We are urged to get our significance (*status* is the popular word) from material goods that others can see—cars, clothes, houses, membership in clubs. How can we avoid being caught up in the rat race of constant getting?

The husband and wife who have chosen spiritual values do not have to seek status by buying more things or competing for attention by means of things. They are secure in each other's love, because that love accepts and approves each of them as persons whose real self is expressed in kindness, concern, and cooperation rather than in competition.

Insecure parents put pressure on their children to achieve, be popular, do everything the neighbors do. Such insecurity can lead to parental pushing of children into activities before they are ready and into dating and sophisticated parties and dances when the children should still be developing at their own pace. Then people worry about adolescents and everyone talks about juvenile delinquency.

The religious family tries to discover what spiritual value is involved in each problem that arises and solve it on that basis. Shall we pass Junior on Cubbing requirements so he can get that next rank with the rest of his den, even if he did do sloppy work? Shall we tell the irate neighbor that Patty didn't pick her flowers? Does Dad boast about the slick deal he pulled? How much do we care about truth?

Should thirteen-year-old Susie go to a formal dance? Shall we get a car like the Jones's or keep building our educational fund? Shall we join the country club or keep up with our church pledge? What are our values?

Because we need the strength that comes from approval of others, the fellowship of the church can support us as we try to hold to what we consider important. Life can be pretty lonely in a materialistic society. Ideally, within the fellowship of the church we share commitment to a deeper search for truth and spiritual values. Since the church is made up of humans, it too often falls short of these aims; sometimes it is not even a loving fellowship, but at least it has such a goal and is struggling toward it.

Granted that we accept religious living as a goal, how can we achieve it? Not in an hour once a week. It requires constant evaluation of living on the basis of moral and ethical values—a God-conscious interpretation of experience. We have to learn to talk together about the meaning of what we do. To the "what" we need to add the "So what?"

Some of this evaluation may come in a time set aside for family worship—if it is real worship, not just a form to go through and get out of the way, like the breakfast dishes. The family that talks over daily happenings, be they the TV show they all watched or a decision to buy a boat, and makes comments and decisions after thinking through the moral principles involved is constantly living religiously. Then marking events with family prayer seems the natural way to relate life to God.

We speak of the kingdom of God and pray for its

coming. Where better than in our own families can we start to work towards it? The family is founded upon giving and receiving love. Here we can love and accept each person, not for what he does but for what he is. We give gladly to each, not according to his contribution but according to his needs, because we love. Here the welfare of each member is as precious to the others as their own, and this is not self-sacrifice but self-realization.

The family is the true religious fellowship, one household in the kingdom of God. Where such families exist, they are truly the leaven in the loaf, for their influence spreads into business, education, government, international affairs—all human life. In what more satisfying way can two lovers find their need for significance met?